God's Secured Treasures
Copyright © 2016 by Samantha T. Maclin-Ware
First Addition: 2016

All rights reserved. No part of this book may be reproduced or transmitted in any form or by any means without written permission of the publisher. Scripture Quotations marked NIV are taken from the NEW INTERNATIONAL VERSION®, NIV® Copyright © 1973, 1978, 1984, 2011 by Biblica, Inc.® Used by permission. All rights reserved worldwide.

Chief Editor: Samantha T. Maclin-Ware
Book cover design: Sean A. Wilson Independent Designer
Layout & Logos: Sean A. Wilson
Photo: Michelle Dokes Photography

ISBN:908-0-692-855508-9
Printed in the United States of America

God's Secured Treasures (Introduction)

What are God's Secured Treasures? The answer is quite simple. These are the rewards that God has stored up or reserved for you to receive according to His perfect will, His prefect way and in His perfect timing throughout your life.

This is December 31st. My first New Year's Eve without my boys. I look at this alone, quiet time as a day to commune with my Lord, to reflect on this past year and step confidently into the new year. For the first time in my life, I will be going to church and assisting with Baptisms at 10 p.m.

You see, I made a silent vow to myself last New Year's Eve to do something different. I felt a strong urge to change my New Year's Eve tradition into something more fulfilling. However, I didn't know last year what that fulfilled agenda would be. There was no better way than to start my new year at church praying for favor and blessings from God to be released in my life and in the lives of my loved ones.

The next morning, I woke up and later went on to Facebook and noticed a repeated message that I couldn't ignore. It stated, "Today, is the 1st day of 365 days. Write your life story." So, I decided to write today being the first day of my work. This was a great way to close one door and step inside a new, opened one.

Last year was a year that I can describe in one word: Preparation. God dealt with me on so many issues like: lack of patience; trusting and loving Him through all circumstances; pleasing Him and not others; loving and showing mercy to others; showing me ways of how great and unconditional His love is for me; receiving His goodness; gaining increase in faith; surrendering every aspect of myself and releasing my fleshy ways to His beautiful will. God, also, removed some people from my life and replaced them with more fulfilling relationships. There were some very difficult moments that truly tested my faith in God, but all along, I trusted Him to know what was best for me. Also, He gave me the ability to heal and opened my heart to recognize new opportunities, dreams and desires.

I'm so grateful for God and his precious, secured treasures that I've received in my life so far. I'm so thankful that God has assigned my Angels to work so diligently and beautifully behind the scenes to manifest my secured treasures and all of God's promises in my life for me and those I love.

It has been both an honor and blessing, but a challenging time because of God's convictions and corrections in my life. God's teachings continue to make me the person He created me to be.

I'm honored to receive even more of God's blessings and treasures that have been stored up and ready to be released because of my prompt obedience to God and having faith and belief in Him and only Him.

As you read, please note that each Bible scripture is subscripted at the beginning of each chapter. The scriptures are ordered and can be found at the end of the book in the "Treasure Resources" Section.

I'm hoping that after reading this book, you will consistently enjoy the beautiful journey that God has planned for you.

Enjoy God's Secured Treasures!!

TABLE OF CONTENTS

Chapter 1: Seek God First……………..........7

Chapter 2: Ask God……………..…………..10

Chapter 3: It's Time to Surrender………......14

Chapter 4: When God Takes Over…………..17

Chapter 5: Love……………………..………...21

Chapter 6: Obeying God Over Sacrifice…....26

Chapter 7: How to Pray And Hearing God….30

Chapter 8: Trusting God…………………..……34

Chapter 9: Thanking God………………….…..38

Chapter 10: Experiencing God's Presence...41

Chapter 11: Never Worry, Doubt Or Fear…..45

Chapter 12: Stepping Out On Faith………….48

Chapter 13: Dreams Come True……………...52

Chapter 14: Waiting On God……………....…..56

Chapter 15: His Way, His Will, ……………….61

Chapter 16: God's Sense Of Humor………...64

Chapter 17: God's Pleasure and Delight…...68

Closing……………...…………………….…..71

End Notes - Treasure Resources…………......75

Acknowledgements………………...………..…..94

Chapter 1

SEEK GOD FIRST

Psalms 37:4[1]
Amos 5:4[2]
Matthew 6:33[3]

For many of my adult years, I went through my daily life going through the motions and not really taking time to bask in God's blessings that He offered me each day. Important life decisions were being made out of order, balance simply did not exist and my life was joyless and fruitless. Once I began my spiritual walk with God, I asked Him the question of why my life seemed to be so chaotic. I recall a morning from waking up from a very thought-provoking dream about God making it very clear to me about putting Him first in my daily life. After that, I began a morning regimen of spending time with God before leaving the house. Currently, I don't leave my home without spending quality time praying, talking and listening to God and reading and studying His word. For me, dedicating this special time means putting God in His rightful place in my life, which is first place. It means all empty voids in my life have now been filled with the love of God. The empty voids that I'm referring to are the lonely heart and overindulgence in eating, drinking, shopping and anything else one tends to do to fill a spot that can only be filled by God. You see, God is a jealous God. He loves you so much and unconditionally. It will truly please Him, if you put and keep Him first place in your life. So, the reality is, you must place God in your life each morning and keep Him close to you throughout your day.

God's Secured Treasures you can expect to receive from Seeking God First:

- ★ Being full of God's love over everything else is the most beautiful feeling.
- ★ You will develop an increased amount of faith in decision making.
- ★ You will expectantly anticipate the fulfillment of God's promises.

Chapter 2

ASK GOD

Matthew 7: 4-8[4]
Matthew 18:19[5]
John 14: 13, 14[6]
James 4:2[7]

    I have a secret to share. God does listen to your prayers and answers them. However, the problem with this truth is that, at times, the results are not what you envision. God doesn't always answer the way you want Him to. Sometimes, He answers you based on your motives.

    I remember a time earlier in my career after completing my Master's program that I was praying consistently for a school to hire me as a school administrator. I had decided all on my own (without God's guidance) to leave a comfortable position as a classroom teacher, with manageable work hours and convenient days and time off, to embark on this new adventure as a school administrator which entailed longer work hours, heavier job duties, having extreme confidence in decision-making, etc. Oh, did I mention that I had two, small children under the age of 4? I thought that it was a blessing from God and rewards of my hard work when I received the news of this job offer. Needless to say, that I only lasted approximately five months in that position. The reasons for the resignation were the excessive workload and lack of manpower. After that ordeal, I had a moment to question God with full reverence as to why this situation didn't work out for me. The answer came to me simply and clearly: my motives were not true. I wanted that job to satisfy my sense of entitlement, not for the glorification of God...My one, true Source. What a light bulb moment that was for me!!!!!! Thank you, Father, for providing me with your Godly understanding!!!!!

Here are a few questions you need to ask yourself while asking God for answers to your prayers. Be sure to provide a true answer to each question.

1. Am I rushing God?
2. Have I forgiven all?
3. Am I comparing myself or situation to others?
4. Am I asking according to God's will and in His perfect timing?
5. Am I asking to please and glorify God?

God's Secured Treasures you can expect to receive while Asking God for answers:

- ★ The mastery of asking God with the right motives is pleasing to Him.
- ★ You will have confidence that the answers to your prayers are on the way in His timing.
- ★ The excitement in knowing that God hears your prayers and will answer them is heavenly.

Chapter 3

IT'S TIME TO SURRENDER

Psalms 37:5[8]
Psalms 55:22[9]
Mark 14:35-36[10]
John 15: 1-8[11]
1 Peter 5:6-10[12]

Have you been trying with all your heart, might and skills to force something to happen? This thing must happen because I say so!! I want it now, my way!! However, the more you try, the more frustrated it becomes because it's not happening according to your timing.

This has happened to me plenty of times and to no avail, I kept finding myself stuck and going around the same mountain as the previous times. This was truly one of the most difficult lessons that God has taught me. You see, I'm the eldest child. My parents instilled in me at an early age the importance of responsibility such as taking care of my younger brother and making good decisions. With this solid foundation, I grew into this, at times, a controlling young woman. I controlled everything and at times tried to control people. I problem solved on my own and forced solutions to the problems. Oh, silly me!!!! How I thought I was in control of it all until one day God made it very clear, "I was nothing without Him." It wasn't until I fell and dropped to my knees and cried out to God to take over it all...my life, my heart, my thoughts, my health, my children, my job, my money, etc. I realized that I couldn't do it on my own anymore. Instantly God told me, "My Darling Daughter, what took you so long to come to me? I've always been here. You're running fast and not making anything happen. Sit, cry and rest and let me comfort you." You know what? I don't know how I knew, but I knew with all my heart that God was speaking to me, and I surrendered all to Him immediately. The more I surrendered to God, the easier it became because I witnessed God working in my life. I'm proud to say that I've been consistently surrendering every aspect of my life to Him, and it has made a positive difference.

God's Secured Treasures you can expect to receive after Surrendering to Him:

- ★ A peace of mind that's beyond understanding will continuously be yours.
- ★ You will develop the ability to enter God's rest and serenity that He has for you.

Chapter 4

WHEN GOD TAKES OVER

Joshua 1:9[13]
Isaiah 41:13[14]

November, 1997 was a joyous time for my family. I found out that I was pregnant with my first child. Everything was going well with the pregnancy until week 20. During a weekend getaway, I felt a stream of water flow like many pregnant women would describe as their "water breaking." However, I was only five months pregnant. This couldn't be what I was feeling. We decided the next morning to go to the emergency room as precaution. It's amazing how life can change in a split second. While at the hospital, the doctor did an ultrasound to check the baby and with astonishment in her eyes, she stated that there was no fluid surrounding my baby. What was she saying? What did this mean? Well, in simple terms, she was stating that due to the lack of fluid, my baby probably would not survive too much longer. Also, that stream of fluid I felt the day before was my water breaking and leaking of amniotic fluid. This leaking would have been perfect to have happened if only I was full-term. So, the doctor decided to admit me to stay in the hospital to watch the baby closely. The next couple of days were very overwhelming. The doctors suggested that we terminate my pregnancy. However, there was one major issue. I was still feeling movement and hearing my baby's heartbeat, which was an indication to me of LIFE. There were a lot of prayers enveloping us during that time from family and close friends and because of that, I will forever be grateful. However, the pivotal moment was when God took over this situation. The doctor peeked his head through the door and asked me if I was ready to be prepped for the termination of my pregnancy. At that very moment, I told him to wait for a moment so I could gather my thoughts. Shortly after, I heard God say, "I placed life in you, and I will take over from this point forward." Prior to this moment, I thought it was us and the doctors who were dictating this situation. I felt deep in my spirit to surrender this ordeal to God, and allowed Him to take over. The doctor returned, and with confidence, I stated my perspective which was to keep my baby and all agreed with support. The journey from that moment to giving birth and postpartum was dramatic, but when God takes over with His Ordainment, there's no amount of negative energy that can stop the blessing from occurring. Needless to say, 18 years later, my healthy, handsome son, Joshua, is on his way to a four-year university. Two years after the birth of Joshua, my second son, Jordan was born healthy and happy. Can we all say together, Won't He do it?!?!?!?!!!!!!!!!!!!!!!

God's Secured Treasures you can expect to receive while Allowing God To Take Over:

★ There's comfort in learning to let go and let God.
★ You will develop confidence in knowing that all will work out for your good regardless of the situation.
★ You will no longer allow stress to invade your life while trying to figure things out on your own.

Chapter 5

LOVE

(God, Self, Others)

Proverbs 31[15]
John 3:16[16]
John 13:14[17]
1 Corinthians 13: 4-8[18]
1 Corinthians 16:14[19]
1 John 4: 7[20]

God loves you unconditionally. Do you REALLY understand what that means? It took me a long time to grasp this concept. Let me explain. God loves you so much that HE sent HIS only earthly son to the cross after enduring so much pain so that each one of you can be free of your sins and have eternal life. Can you imagine, giving up your child, pet or a loved one to die for people you don't know? God loves you so much that any mistakes you make, he turns them around for your good. All He asks of you is to love Him, believe in Him, follow His commandments and to love others. He has promised you so much in return as rewards. God is such a good, good God!!!!!

As God continues to love you, He teaches you how to love yourself. To see yourself in the same loving manner as He sees you is such a remarkable revelation. This was another concept that I had a difficult time understanding. Through many intimate moments with God, I was finally able to discern how God wanted me to love myself. You see, you are valuable, worthy and deserving of the best!!! According to Proverbs 31, you're far more worthy than the precious stone of the ruby. You must meditate on that statement and believe it for yourself. After the realization, you will increase your faith in God to direct you to positive opportunities and surround you with loving people who will also love you by your worth. Which brings me to my third point of LOVE.

Loving others can be challenging at times. To please God, you must love others. How can this be done, if someone close to you betrays you? Always remember that God puts others in your life sometimes for a season or longer. The ones who are in your life for a season, simply, love them enough to lovingly let them go and look at the cycle as a lesson learned. Yes, there are lessons to be learned from someone's betrayal. Go within and look at your truth. Closed doors are blessings because they lead to open doors full of new opportunities. Your spirit may be crushed because God decided unexpectedly to remove a person from your life. This happens to us all at different stages in our lives. Recently, God started making shifts in my relationships. Some of the shifts, I clearly understood the reasoning for the removal of the individuals. Whether the reason was from outgrowing each other or betrayal, I had to pray consistently to God for forgiveness and allow myself to surrender these relationships to Him. In other relationships, I had no idea why God was removing the individuals away from me. After much prayer, I realized that, at times, God shifts people away from you because they are not equipped to go to that higher level that HE has secured for you. One thing is certain, whoever and whatever God removes from your life, HE replaces it with much better!!!!!!! I can truly attest that for every person that God has lovingly removed from my life, He has replaced them with beautiful, loving genuine individuals. Keep God first and at the center of all your relationships and remember that Love is the key to happiness.

God's Secured Treasures you can expect to receive When You Love God, Yourself and Others:

- ★ Trusting God with your relationships is rewarding.
- ★ You will always do what's right because love is the foundation of your reasoning.
- ★ You will feel the beautiful sensation of love and how it overflows in all your relationships.

Chapter 6

OBEYING GOD OVER SACRIFICE

Exodus 19:5[21]
Deuteronomy 11:1[22]
Romans 1:5[23]
James 1:25[24]

One of the most difficult decisions I ever had to make in my adult life was to leave a marriage that no longer served a purpose for my life. Everyone who decides to marry has the intentions of taking their vows seriously and the marriage lasting forever. When things are going well, marriage is the most beautiful experience. However, when things are not so good, it can become one of the most challenging experiences you ever have to deal with in life. Marriage is a difficult task, and it requires hard work and much effort from both individuals. There will be many obstacles a couple will face throughout the duration of their marriage from financial and medical issues and raising children to infidelity and lack and loss of love and respect which happen to be my experiences in my previous marriage. However, the key is for both individuals to want to work hard and try to salvage the marriage. In my opinion, many marriages don't work because of the following reason: wrong motives for getting married. For instance, your circle of friends is getting married, not taking the time to date and getting to know your partner long enough to truly develop unconditional love, lack of self-love, self-indulging and immaturity and most important, not keeping God first place in the marriage. So, after years of being in a dysfunctional marriage and trying to make it work, I had a very long and intimate conversation with God. One day, I sat at the foot of my bed and God spoke to me about trusting Him to leave my marriage. I decided to obey God instead of holding on to all the sacrifices I made in the marriage such as owning a house, having children and other conveniences. Many may believe that God will never tell His daughter to leave a marriage after making the vows and having two children; however, God doesn't want His daughter to live a life other than it being lived with fulfillment and joy that only He can provide. Again, it was the hardest decision I ever had to make. That was one time, I heard from God and took a giant leap of faith and everything lined up divinely. Of course, there were some difficulties, but God has a way of giving you both strength and perseverance to push through to victory. Later, I took the alone, peaceful time as a blessing to get to know me and work on myself so that I can be a better partner in my next relationship. It was also mandatory for me to provide love and stability for my children. I now have a new title of being a single mother, and I wear it proudly. I can attest that there can be a beautiful life after divorce filled with God's treasures. My, ex and I, with a lot of prayer and patience have been able to maintain a healthy and respectful relationship. The rewards of favor you receive from God after obeying Him is amazing!!! Thank you and Glory to God!!!!!

God's Secured Treasures you can expect to receive When You Obey God:

★ You will wake up every day full of jubilation knowing that you're doing all things to please God.
★ You will feel confident in listening to God's personal will for you instead of abiding in man-made laws.

Chapter 7

HOW TO PRAY AND HEARING FROM GOD

Matthews 6:5-13[25]
John 14:1-31[26]
Ephesians 6:18[27]
Philippians 4:6[28]
1 Thessalonians 5:17[29]
1 John 5:14[30]

It's so refreshing to know that God is always available and with you. To our simplistic minds, it may be difficult for some to believe this. It shouldn't be too much of a challenge to reach out to God when you are in need, but somehow, you tend to make this a difficult practice. Prayer can be defined as a very long testament to God, repeating His Word/Promises from scripture, having an intimate conversation with God alone in the comforts of your home, a formal prayer during church service with others, or a simple 2-3 words statement such as, "Thank you, Father." You can speak your prayer aloud, in a whisper, in your mind or through reactions such as tears. Nothing is too big or too small of a challenge or too much of a sin for our God. God sees and knows you. He is happy that you are communicating with Him in any way that brings you comfort.

    I will share a few personal prayer experiences in my beautiful walk with God. For instance, when I wake up each morning, I immediately say good morning to God and thank Him for a peaceful night's rest and waking me up. Believe or not, that's a prayer, and you're seeking God first. It's that simple. After that, I usually wake up an hour early to spend some quiet time with God reading my Bible and meditating on His word. The important key is to create the time that is comforting to you and your lifestyle. Also, I pray to God throughout my day. Sometimes, I speak with Him in my head saying a simple thank you, or I'm asking Him for help with me or someone else. Yes, I do make it a practice to pray for others because it pleases God in doing so. God will reward you when you do. Once, you begin to experience God's answers to your prayers, you will routinely pray without putting in much effort.

After you've mastered the precious art of prayer, hearing from God is equally as important. God speaks to you in many ways depending on how He sees what's best for you at the time. You must be still, listen and be prepared to hear from God. Some ways He speaks to you during or after prayer is through emotions such as peace and/or zeal, your emotional feeling after speaking with God about your situation, through His silence (delay doesn't mean denial or objection), and in your conscience (the deep knowing). Other ways He speaks to you are through loved ones, a smile from a stranger, messages and dreams and through His word (the Bible).

God's Secured Treasures you can expect to receive When You Pray and Hear From God:

- ★ You will experience an overwhelming feeling of peace and confidence.
- ★ You will develop boldness in knowing and doing what's best for you.
- ★ Through practice and having awareness, you will receive an amazing amount of wisdom from God.

Chapter 8

TRUSTING GOD

Genesis 22:1-14[31]
Psalms 37:3-6[32]
Psalms 46:10[33]
Psalms 91[34]
Psalms 118:6[35]
Proverbs 3:5[36]

One of the biggest challenges in my walk with God was letting go and trusting God in all aspects of my life. I don't know why we tend to think we are strong, powerful and smart enough to handle our own situations. Then we wonder why nothing is going well in our lives. However, after making many mistakes, I learned that trusting God is the only way to live the prosperous life that God has intended for all of us to live. My motto that I live faithfully by is trusting only in God's perfect will, way and timing with everything in my life. Without my help (relying on self instead of God), God can move in my life and provide blessings, provision and protection in abundance to me and my loved ones. For instance, after completing my student teaching in December, 1994, I was so worried about the next step in life and that was finding a job. In hindsight, I realize that the enemy whispered lies to me and made me question if anyone was going to hire a first-year teacher in the middle of the school year. All my trust was in self and not in God to take care of this situation. I felt defeated, sad and was questioning what I thought to be my passion, which was becoming a teacher. I said a simple silent prayer to God to help me. Finally, I had to let go of the situation because it was starting to consume me. I decided to take the two-week holiday break to rest, and in January, I would begin to look for a teaching position. Then, the unthinkable took place. I received a phone call over the two week break from a high school principal who received some favorable accolades from my supervising teacher who presided over me while I student taught. He wanted me to come in for an interview for a teaching position that would be opening in the month of January. What?!?!?!?!?!!!!!! I couldn't believe it!!! I didn't have to look for this, it came to me. My excitement shortly turned into doubt because I started worrying (not trusting God) about how well I would do in the interview. The day came for the interview. I went in as confident as I was back then and was introduced to a female assistant principal and realized that this was not the principal, the person, I spoke with on the telephone. So, I followed the assistant to her office, and we proceeded with small talk. She then made a statement that blew me anyway. She stated that she had read my resume, saw that I was qualified for the position and noticed that she and I were members of the same sorority. At that moment, the appointment was no longer a job interview, but a conversation with her offering me the position. Wonderful!!!!!!! You see, you simply have to trust God regardless of what the situation looks like, what people may say or what you think is true. Keep in mind that God has already worked out your situation in the best possible way for you. If it's God's will, he will make a way. You must Trust Him!!!

God's Secured Treasures you can expect to receive When You Trust in God:

★ You never have to worry, doubt or fear because you have put your trust in God.
★ Trusting God is the ultimate answer to your prayers.
★ You will have the ability to freely release all that burdens you.
★ God will always take care of you.

Chapter 9

THANKING GOD

Psalms 24:8-10[37]
Psalms 95:1-11[38]
Psalms 107:1[39]
Isaiah 25:1[40]
Ephesians 5:20[41]
1 Thessalonians 5:18[42]

I'm thankful for God for giving me HIS wisdom and knowledge to write these messages to you. I'm so thankful for God's goodness in all aspects of my life. For a very long time, I would get up each morning and move forward with my day's activities and not realize all the good that God was providing for me and my family. Now, during my walk with God, there isn't a day that goes by without me thanking Him for all His blessings: big and small. A few things that I thank God for are waking me up each morning from a restful night's sleep, having perfect health, the sweet smell of a baby, finding a parking spot close to the entrance of a building on a rainy day, being able to eat a hot slice of pizza the moment I truly have a taste for it, walking into my home from being out on a very hot day or extremely cold day and being blessed with air conditioning and heat, the beautiful, abundant blessing of pure, clean water to drink, wash and cook with, the blessing of having God's peace in protecting me from things unbeknownst to me, the ability to share an encouraging word to someone at the proper time, having His grace, mercy and favor over my life; even though, I don't deserve it; simply because He loves me so much, having the ability to give to the less fortunate and never having to worry, doubt or fear anyone or anything because God has promised to always provide and protect me. Lastly, I'm so thankful for God's love for me because it was only through Him that I could love myself and others. I'm quite sure I left out many more important items and situations to be thankful for; however, I'm sure you can relate to all of God's goodness that He has exhibited throughout your lives as well. God is truly a good, good God!!!!!

God's Secured Treasures you can expect to receive When You Thank God:

- ★ God is amused of your love for Him while thanking Him for all things.
- ★ More blessings are on the way because of your acknowledgement of Him.
- ★ God enjoys when you praise Him aloud.

Chapter 10

EXPERIENCING GOD'S PRESENCE

Exodus 33:14[43]
Psalms 27:13[44]
Jeremiah 29:13[45]
Matthew 5:8[46]
Hebrews 13:8[47]

I remember the very first time in my life that I felt God's presence. First, let me explain what God's presence means. It's a feeling or knowing you get in certain situations that envelopes your soul which feels like peace, love or comfort or a combination all three. I can recall the time when I was completing the final step in receiving my Master's Degree, and I had to present my final project orally to a panel of college professors. In this meeting, which is called a Capstone, they asked me questions regarding my work, and I had to prove my perspective. I had done all my research to complete the task; however, I was very nervous. On the morning of my Capstone experience, my mother, always being my greatest encourager, shared with me some personal, encouraging words and gave me a daily inspirational reading to take with me. The message simply stated to believe in myself and how God didn't bring me this far to leave or fail me. It's amazing how powerful it is to hear God's word especially for you at the most perfect time. So, I arrived early, and as I waited for the person before me to complete his appointment, I read and meditated on those beautiful, inspiring words that my mother gave to me. Finally, one of the professors called me in. I felt at that moment that God's presence was taking over me. Of course, at that time, I didn't know what it was because it was before my intense walk with God. However, knowing what I know now, it was God's presence that I was experiencing. I felt an abundant amount of peace and confidence that I could not have prepared or created on my own. God spoke through me to my professors and the experience shifted from worry, doubt and fear to confidence, contentment and peace. The professors expressed their positive feedback. I couldn't believe the experience was over. I felt I had more knowledge of my perspective to share with them. It was one of the most exhilarating experiences of my life.

God's presence is such a beautiful feeling, and it can come in many forms. Sometimes I feel His presence with a sense of peace and positive energy such as I previously discussed. On the other hand, after prayer, I feel His presence in an overwhelming emotional manner that surpasses understanding that can feel like an abundant amount of elation, zeal or happiness. Remember this very important note, to experience God's presence, you have to pray, be still and know that God Is the Great I Am.

God's Secured Treasures you can expect to receive When You Experience God's Presence:

- ★ An astounding sense of peace will overtake you.
- ★ It's comfort in knowing that you're always being kept safely by God.
- ★ By having child-like faith, you will find comfort from God to handle life's situations.

Chapter 11

NEVER WORRY, DOUBT OR FEAR

Psalms 34:4[48]
Psalms 91[49]
Isaiah 35:4[50]
Matthew 21:21[51]
John 14:27[52]
Romans 8: 38-39[53]
Hebrews 11:1-40[54]
James 1:6[55]

I believe that whatever you're worried about is usually the opposite of what is happening. Worry is simply a disguise; not real at all. So, knowing this, why do you waste time worrying, doubting or fearing anyone or anything? In every one of my life's experiences, I can honestly say that all things worked out well for my good. I only had to stop, pray and believe that God will work everything out with perfection. There were times I would worry about my finances, and then later I would suddenly receive a gift or money in the most miraculous way and at the most perfect time. There was a time when I doubted things would work out with the buying and selling of my homes. I was doubtful if I could find a buyer and a new place at consecutive times. Through prayer and my dependence on God, the closings took place within just two weeks of one another...perfect timing. Lastly, I remember a time when my central air unit would not work properly and finding out that the only thing needed was the replacement of a fuse. Of course, these are small occurrences, but it's in the small blessings that prepare you for the larger blessings such as a loved one's state of health taking a turn from worst to a miraculous recovery. There will be times that your faith will be tested in huge ways with serious situations, and that is when you must turn to God to give you His Godly strength and courage through your weakest moments of worry, doubt and fear. On the other side of it all will be a very powerful victory with your name on it.

God's Secured Treasure you can expect to receive When You Never Worry, Doubt or Fear:

- ★ There's comfort in knowing that God has your back.
- ★ The ability to enjoy your life while God is working behind the scenes is truly a blessing.

Chapter 12

STEPPING OUT ON FAITH

Psalms 46:10[56]
Mark 11:22-24[57]
John 20:29[58]
Romans 10:17[59]
Philippians 4:13[60]
Hebrews 11: 1-6[61]

As I write this section, I hear such quotes in my head like, "keep the faith," "God can do the impossible" and "believe in the invisible." It's difficult to do, but I'm trying my best to truly believe these things when I don't know what steps I'm going to take after the completion of this book. Believe me when I say that this is a time when I'm truly stepping out on faith believing God to guide me into the direction of the right paths of divine relationships and interventions. "Thy Will Be Done" is what I meditate on daily.

You see, this is not the very first time that I'm believing God for something and stepping out on faith. This is just one of many. For instance, I can recall when I first realized that I was afraid of public speaking. I was in 8th grade and as the class vice-president, I had the honors of introducing a very popular Chicago news reporter at that time. I was petrified to stand and speak in front of my classmates, parents and teachers. I practiced my speech a million times at home looking in the mirror, in front of my teddy bears (yes, I was still fond of teddy bears in 8th grade) and in front of my family, but nothing compared to speaking in front of a large audience. Then came the moment where I had to speak publicly. Since, I got up and stepped out on faith, all went well after speaking the first few words. Now, let's fast forward to my adult years. I can recall some pretty, scary moments that I was placed in, and all I could do and had left was to step out on faith. There were times where I realized stepping out on faith was better than being miserable in a situation. Anything would've been better than where I was at that time. Usually, this referred to me shifting positions in my career, choosing healthier relationships and/or making important life decisions with material items and what was best for my boys.

The best advice that I can give you when trying to make a very important decision by stepping out on faith is to always, always, always pray first!!!!!!!!!!!!!!! Once you're quiet and willing to wait on God to answer you and you're confident that you've heard from Him, then go ahead and step out on faith. Two things can happen after this occurs. One, your choice is the best one and you move towards your victory that's ordained by God especially for you. Or, you step out on faith thinking that you heard from God, but the outcome was a mistake. Don't fret if this happens. What I can promise you is that if you make a mistake, God can turn your mistake around for your good. God always looks at your heart. If your heart is pure while stepping out on faith, then God will provide for you. He is able to make all things possible.

God's Secured Treasures you can expect to receive When You Step Out On Faith:

★ There's confidence in knowing a new door is opening for you.
★ There's confidence in knowing if you make a mistake, God will turn it around to work in your favor.

Chapter 13

DREAMS COME TRUE

Psalms 5:12[62]
Isaiah 58:11[63]
Jeremiah 29:11[64]
Amos 9:13[65]
Matthew 19:26[66]
Luke 18:27[67]
1 Corinthians 2:9[68]
Ephesians 3:20[69]

    Did you know that everything you see, touch and use started as a simple thought in the inventor or creator's mind? Also, did you know that God places dreams and desires in you to bring them to manifestation, if you don't give up? So how do you know if the desire that's been placed inside you is from God or from your carnal self? Here's one way to know. If you've prayed and asked God for clarification and/or revelation and you've noticed a consistent number of signs, or some may call them coincidences, that motivate you to continue on your journey, then there's a good chance that you are on your way to fulfilling your life purpose.

When I was in high school, I always had a dream of going away to college. I always knew that I would fulfill this dream without knowing the details as to where or how it was going to happen; I just knew it. During this time, God had made many arrangements for me to witness close family members who attended college and were very successful in their plight. Also, my favorite television show at that time was A Different World which chronicled the lives of college aged students living on a college campus. These were all great examples that God used in His divine timing to motivate me to work hard at my dream of going to and graduating from college.

There were many other times in my life that God placed dreams and desires in my heart. Most of them, I never knew the desire was in me until God started exposing me to the ideas. For instance, God has placed both short and long term desires in me to pursue from taking exotic, international vacations, to becoming inducted into my sorority to receiving advanced degrees and having two children. Each of these dreams came true for me because they were ordained by God. He provided every single blessing with provision that was needed for my dreams to come true. There are many beautiful things about God, but one is His wonderful way of orchestrating your life. God has a bird's eye view of each one of your lives from preconception to eternal life. It is truly remarkable how God has planned your life in the most meticulous way from His divine connections, timing and interventions to manifesting your dreams to completion. My advice to you is to never give up on your dreams. If you are constantly thinking of a particular idea, this may be God's way of trying to get your attention. God wants you all to live happy, healthy and prosperous lives. However, you must get into agreement with Him, stay true to yourself and cooperate with Him all the way through to the manifestation of your dreams. Trust me, you will not be disappointed.

God's Secured Treasures you can expect to receive When Your Dreams Come True:

- ★ There's proof that God answers prayers abundantly.
- ★ There's confirmation that if God blesses you once, He will do it again.
- ★ God will abundantly, manifest your dreams and fulfill His promises to you, if you obey, believe and trust in Him.
- ★ Continue to bless and worship God after your dreams come true.

Chapter 14

WAITING ON GOD OR IS GOD WAITING ON YOU?

Psalms 27:14[70]
Isaiah 40:31[71]
Habakkuk 2:3[72]
Galatians 6:9[73]
Ephesians 2:10[74]

Another one of my struggles in my walk with God is patiently waiting on God to move in His timing instead of my timing. I must admit that having patience or lack of patience has been one of the most difficult lessons I had to learn from God. What I've learned from this lesson is that

God loves me too much to give me what I've been praying for before I'm ready to receive it. So, what do you tend to do while you wait? You get frustrated, refuse to enjoy the small blessings that God gives you daily, let doubt, worry and unbelief settle in your mind and don't aggressively prepare for what you're asking for. However, I have great news for you from my personal experience. What you should do while waiting on God's victory in your life is to allow Him to do a thorough work in and through you. Allow Him to build your character by polishing your traits of love, peace, joy, patience and being merciful towards others. Allow God to love you so that you will learn how to properly love Him back, yourself and others. Allow God to show you how to have fun and give you time alone to tap into your creativity and passions. Allow God to take His time to heal you in all the areas that need to be healed. It's also important to note, that during this period of waiting on God, you must give yourself a break if you make mistakes and practice patience if you feel that your blessings are not happening fast enough. This is a step by step method of how God works in your life. Progression is a process and takes time. Waiting is a part of life, and at the end of the wait is always victory. So, rejoice in the period of waiting.

On the other hand, what happens when God waits on you? I remember when God placed a desire in me to write a book. However, it became a problem when I tried to write a fictional book that was not ordained by God's perfect timing. The problem I faced was that the more I wrote, the more my writing seemed inauthentic in that genre. Later, I had an intimate discussion with God asking Him what I was doing wrong, and He simply stated, "Nonfiction." I immediately tabled the original project. Honestly, it took me some time to begin to write this one. I procrastinated because I wasn't confident in myself to take on the task. After some time, I began to consistently write the material for this book. It was a blessing, that as I wrote each chapter, how simply the information appeared in my mind. I knew wholeheartedly that this was one of many blessings given to me that was ordained by God.

As I look back, I realized that it's not us always waiting on God, but at times, it's God waiting on us. You see, delay doesn't mean denial. He denied me the ability to write the first book I had attempted to write to make me spend more time in preparation (researching, taking online classes, personal interviews, etc.), but then the time had come for me to write, but in His perfect way and timing. God makes you wait at times for reasons known to Him, but there are times when He shows up and expects you to be obedient to Him in His timing. Many times, you get so used to waiting that when God shows up unexpectedly giving you great ideas, you don't act immediately because of fears and doubts. The blessing of it all is that regardless if God is waiting on you or if you are waiting on God, the situation will manifest itself in the most beautiful, God ordained way.

God's Secured Treasures you can expect to receive from Waiting On God:

- ★ God's tardiness doesn't mean He has forgotten about you.
- ★ Rest assure, that while waiting, God is preparing you for bigger and better opportunities.
- ★ Waiting builds your character, strength and patience.

Chapter 15

HIS WILL, HIS WAY, HIS PERFECT TIMING

Ecclesiastes 3:11[75]
Isaiah 40:31[76]
Habakkuk 2:3[77]
Matthew 19:26[78]
Romans 12:12[79]
Galatians 6:9[80]

Have you ever developed a perfect plan for your day, only to have an unexpected interruption take place? I'm sure no one is happy when this happens. However, you can look at this situation in another way. God knows and sees things that are invisible to us. God being the loving God that He is will always protect you. At times, that may mean for you to alter your plans that you worked on so diligently. Let me give you an example. My girlfriends and I were researching villa accommodations for our St. Lucia vacation and came across this magnificent villa. We all agreed that we loved this one particular place and had planned to make the deposit. Shortly after a conversation with the contact person of the villa, she informed us that the owners had suddenly decided to sell the villa. So, the villa was no longer available for vacation rental. Of course, we were heartbroken when we heard the news because of the wasted time that was spent searching for the perfect vacation villa. It was shortly after that, I realized and felt deep in my spirit and, not knowing the details, that God was saving us from something. Was He saving us from an unsafe community, being in the tropics, an infestation of bugs of some sort (that would have freaked us out) or the villa not being in its' best condition? What I know to be a fact is that we are always safe when we place God in charge of every aspect of our lives, yes, including vacation planning. Since, we were all obedient to God and allowed Him to work His perfect will, way and timing in our lives, the vacation happened to be the best vacation I had ever experienced. The villa we ended up staying at was even more beautiful and had more amenities than the first one. You see, when God takes away something whether it's an idea, a material thing, a person or a situation, He always replaces it with someone or something bigger and/or better. When you pray, be sure to always ask God's help according to His perfect will, way and timing. You will never be disappointed. God is our Only, True Source!

God's Secured Treasures you can expect to receive when You are in the will of God and doing things His way and in His perfect timing:

- ★ You're safe and secure; no worries, no matter what.
- ★ Receive God's precious blessings by believing that He is our One, True Source.

Chapter 16

GOD'S SENSE OF HUMOR

Job 5:22[81]
Psalms 2:4[82]
Psalms 59:8[83]
Proverbs 17:22[84]
Proverbs 31:25[85]

God must have a sense of humor to deal with us, His children, daily. As I write this, I have a smile on my face thinking of quite a few times I know God got a chuckle from some of my acts. For instance, I was expecting a breakthrough to occur in my life. Prior to the breakthrough, God gave me signs to keep me encouraged and to strive for His promises. So, I received a very strong confirming sign from God, but not quite the manifestation that I was hoping for. Remember,

God works in His way, His will and His perfect timing which is in many cases quite differently than how you anticipate it to occur. Anyway, back to my confirming sign, I almost passed out with excitement from the news. I, also, remember God speaking to me at that same moment, "My daughter, the way you just responded to the sign tells me that you're not quite ready for a full manifestation, but continue to prepare for what you're asking me for." I imagined God smiling down on me at my response to His sign.

Also, I can recall the time when my kids were learning to drive. Both asked me for the keys to my car when they felt they were ready to drive. The key words here are **they felt ready**. However, the reality was that I knew for a fact they weren't ready. Joshua had trouble with accelerating too fast while making rights turns, and Jordan displayed the same heavy foot action each time he accelerated. Needless, to say, it was one of those moments my children caused me to have much anxiety. The sense of humor here is that many times we feel ready, but God sees and knows we are not. So, He smiles at us just like I smiled at my boys. I knew with practice and preparation, they will eventually become great drivers, but not before. I did not give them the keys before they were ready, just like God makes us wait until we are ready for the treasures He has for us.

Another way that God displays His sense of humor is toward the enemy. God is the great I AM!!!! He is Everything!!!!! There is nothing or no one that is above Him. Of course, He laughs at the enemy when he tries to come against Him and His children. We, as God's children, need to take on that same action which is laughter, when the enemy tries to attack us. We need to laugh because he's already defeated. The victory is already won for us. All we need to do is keep our faith and belief in God, and God will be sure to rescue us with a smile. God promises us that no weapon that the enemy tries to attack us with will ever prosper. It's great news for us to know, and it is truly a blessing that God is lovingly smiling down on us with His sense of humor and laughing at the enemy's moves.

God's Secured Treasures you can expect to receive When You Witness God's Sense of Humor:

- ★ Lighten up, God loves you.
- ★ It's okay to laugh at yourself; sense of humor gives you peace.
- ★ The victory has already been won for you.

Chapter 17

GOD'S PLEASURE AND DELIGHT IN YOU

Psalms 149:4[86]
Jeremiah 1:5[87]
Zephaniah 3:17[88]
Luke 12:32[89]
Romans 8:37[90]
1 Corinthians 2:9[91]
Galatians 5: 22-23[92]
Revelation 21:4[93]

God's love for you is so grand and unconditional that many of us cannot grasp how massive this concept is with our human mind. It's truly a blessing that God chose you and wants you to enjoy every single day of your life. Regardless of the circumstances that take place in your life, because of His grace and mercy, we can enjoy His presence and favor during our storms. No matter what mistakes you've made or sins you committed, God loves you!! He takes pleasure in you and your well-being and delights in you. God sees you in your purest form. You are His special creation that He meticulously formed into His image. His plan for your life is bigger and more rewarding than you can ever imagine. He already knows the mistakes you will make and the great deeds that you will display before you think of them. However, you never have to worry about the mistakes or the sins because according to God's promises, all we need to do as His children is to acknowledge Him, repent of our sins and believe that we are forgiven. That's when you will see how delighted God is in you when He takes your wrongs and turn them around for your good.

    There are so many ways that God shows His pleasure and delight in you. For instance, it pleases God every time you exhibit a good act or deed to help others, spending alone time with Him, praying for others, just being your true, authentic self, learning from your mistakes, and not taking anyone or anything for granted just to name a few.

How wonderful it is for the Great I AM to be delighted in you. If God takes pleasure and delight in you, it doesn't matter who is against you.

God's Secured Treasures you can expect to receive when you feel God's Pleasure and Delight in You:

- ★ You are the apple of God's eye.
- ★ God created you in His image.
- ★ God loves you unconditionally.

In Closing...

Numbers 6:24-26[94]

    In conclusion, God is the Great I Am!!! God is so good. God loves us all unconditionally. We can surrender all our worries, doubts and fears to God. Remember, fear is only an illusion. The only true emotion is the love of God. God doesn't ask much from us as His children. All He wants us to do is love Him with all our hearts and to love others. If we do this, all other life's dilemmas will be fairly easy to solve because we will have faith and trust in God to give us the strength that's needed to get through each moment of our lives.

    Many may ask how we can develop an intimate relationship with God and feel His presence and receive the secured treasures that he has stored for us. Well, let me share my profound, yet, simple experience with you. A few years ago, my life was making major shifts due to unforeseen circumstances. Nothing or no one was filling this unexplainable void that was taking place within myself. I felt deep in my soul a fascination with scripture and God's word. However, I really didn't know where to begin. God was leading and guiding my steps to Him in His most divine way and timing. I started reading small daily, inspirational works that were helping me to understand God's words and messages. Then, I felt a desperate need to read the Bible, which I knew would give me a deeper meaning of God's words and answers to my prayers. However, I was hesitant to take on the task because of the complexity of the material. Around the same time, a friend suggested that I should start reading the Book of Proverbs in the Bible. The Book of Proverbs is composed up of 31 chapters with insightful information regarding practical occurrences of life. So, I began by reading one chapter a day. The more I read, the more I wanted to read. From there, I read the Book of Psalms in the Bible. The material in this Book is compiled of short poems, prayers or songs. From there, I found a church that I love. I paid attention to the sermons the Pastors spoke about and went home and studied the material in the Bible. I became so passionate about God and His word that I decided on a daily schedule that incorporated intimate time with Him in His presence, reading and studying His word. For you to have an intimate relationship with God, you must look at your personal lifestyle and dedicate time to Him that's conducive to your schedule. My schedule looks like this on most days. I wake up at 5 a.m. and spend about 45 minutes with God praying, reading His word and basking in His presence. Throughout my day, I'm constantly doing check-in's with God by saying simple, quick prayers of thank you's, I love you's and praise and worships. In the evening, I spend more quiet time with Him worshipping Him, reading and/or looking at a spiritual program on TV. Please keep in my mind, that this is my personal schedule with God. Surprisingly, I still have plenty of time left to take care of my business and enjoy all that life has to offer. He created each of us to be different. So, as you begin and continue your spiritual journey with God, he will lead you in the most intimate, personal manner and help you organize a schedule that works best for you and Him.

Your spiritual journey will be an amazing one. Be sure to take each day at a time and bask in the blissful ways of life that God has created especially for you.

Enjoy receiving God's Secured Treasures that He has stored up especially for you while on your spiritual journey.

As I close, I leave you with one of my favorite Bible scriptures that displays God's promises to us.

"The Lord bless you and watch, guard and keep you. The Lord make His face to shine upon you and enlighten you and be gracious to you. The Lord lift up His countenance upon you and give you peace."

Numbers 6:24-26, NIV

ENDNOTES:
Treasure Resources

CHAPTER 1: Seek God First

1. "Delight yourself in the Lord, and He will give you the desires of your heart."
Psalms 37:4 (NIV)
2. "Seek Me and live." Amos 5:4 (NIV)
3. "But seek first His kingdom and righteousness, and all these things will be given to you as well." Matthew 6:33 (NIV)

CHAPTER 2: Ask God

4. "Ask and it will be given to you; seek and you will find; knock and the door will be opened to you. For everyone who asks, receives; he who seeks, finds; and to him who knocks, the door will be opened." Matthew 7: 4-8 (NIV)

5. "Again, I tell you that if two of you on earth agree about anything you ask for, it will be done for you by my father in heaven."
Matthew 18:19 (NIV)

6. "And I will do whatever you ask in my name, so that the Son may bring glory to the Father. You may ask me for anything in my name, and I will do it." John 14:13, 14 (NIV)

7. "You want something but don't get it. You kill and covet, but you cannot have what you want. You quarrel and fight. You do not have, because you do not ask God." James 4:2 (NIV)

CHAPTER 3: It's Time to Surrender

8. "Commit your way to the Lord; trust in Him and he will bring to pass."
Psalms 37:5 (KJV)

9. "Cast your cares on the Lord and He will sustain you; he will never let righteousness fall."
Psalms 55:22 (NIV)

10. "Going a little farther, he fell to the ground and prayed that if possible the hour might pass from him. Father, he said. Take this cup from me. Yet not what I will, but what you will."
Mark 14: 35-36 (NIV)
11. "I am the true vine, and my Father is the gardener..." John 15:1-8 (NIV)
12. "Humble yourselves, therefore, under God's mighty hand, that he may lift you up in due time. Cast all your anxiety on him because he cares for you..." 1 Peter 5: 6-10 (NIV)

CHAPTER 4: When God Takes Over

13. "Have I not commanded you? Be strong and courageous, for the Lord your God will be with you wherever you go." Joshua 1:9 (NIV)
14. "For I am the Lord, your God, who takes hold of your right hand and says to you, Do not fear; I will help you." Isaiah 41:13 (NIV)

CHAPTER 5: Love

15. "The words of King Lemuel - an oracle his mother taught him…" Proverbs 31 (NIV)

16. "For God so loved the world that he gave his one and only son that whoever believes in him shall not perish but have eternal life."
John 3:16 (NIV)

17. "Now that I, your Lord and Teacher, have washed your feet, you also should wash one another's feet." John 13:14 (NIV)

18. "Love is patient, love is kind. It does not envy, it does not boast, it is not proud…"
1 Corinthians 13: 4-8 (NIV)

19. "Do everything in love."
1 Corinthians 16:14 (NIV)

20. "Dear friends, let us love one another, for love comes from God. Everyone who loves has been born of God and knows God."
1 John 4:7 (NIV)

CHAPTER 6: Obeying God Over Sacrifice

21. "Now therefore, if ye will obey my voice indeed, and keep my covenant, then ye shall be a peculiar treasure unto me above all people: for all the earth is mine."
Exodus 19:5 (KJV)

22. "Love the Lord your God and keep his requirements, his decrees, his laws and his commands always." Deuteronomy 11:1 (NIV)

23. "Through him and for his name's sake, we received grace and apostleship to call people from among all the Gentiles to the obedience that comes from faith." Romans 1:5 (NIV)

24. "But the man who looks intently into the perfect law that gives freedom, and continues to do this, not forgetting what he has heard, but doing it - he will be blessed in what he does."
James 1:25 (NIV)

CHAPTER 7: How to Pray and Hearing from God

25. "But when you pray, go into your room, close the door and pray to your Father, who is unseen..." Matthew 6: 5-13 (NIV)
26. "Do not let your hearts be troubled. Trust in God; trust also in me..." John 14: 1-31 (NIV)
27. "And pray in the Spirit on all occasions with all kinds of prayers and requests. With this in mind, be alert and always keep on praying for all the saints." Ephesians 6:18 (NIV)
28. "Do not be anxious about anything, but in everything, by prayer and petition, with thanksgiving present your requests to God." Philippians 4:6 (NIV)
29. "Pray continually."
1 Thessalonians 5:17 (NIV)
30. "This is the confidence we have in approaching God: that if we ask anything according to his will, he hears us."
1 John 5:14 (NIV)

CHAPTER 8: Trusting God

31. "Some time later God tested Abraham. He said to him, Abraham! Here I am, he replied..." Genesis 22:1-14 (NIV)

32. "Trust in the Lord and do good; dwell in the land and enjoy safe pasture. Delight yourself in the Lord and he will give you the desires of your heart. Commit your way to the Lord trust in him and he will do this." Psalms 37:3-6 (NIV)

33. "Be still, and know that I am God; I will be exalted among the nations, I will be exalted in the earth." Psalms 46:10 (NIV)

34. "He who dwells in the shelter of the Most High will rest in the shadow of the Almighty..." Psalms 91 (NIV)

35. "The Lord is with me; I will not be afraid." Psalms 118:6 (NIV)

36. "Trust in the Lord with all your heart and lean not on your understanding." Proverbs 3:5 (NIV)

CHAPTER 9: Thanking God

37. "Who is this King of glory? The Lord strong and mighty, the Lord mighty in battle. Lift up your heads, O you gates; lift them up, you ancient doors, that the King of glory may come. Who is he, this king of glory? The Lord Almighty - he is the King of glory." Psalms 24: 8-10 (NIV)
38. "Come, let us sing for the joy of the Lord; let us shout aloud to the Rock of our salvation..." Psalms 95:1-11 (NIV)
39. "Give thanks to the Lord; for he is good." Psalms 107:1 (NIV)
40. "O Lord, you are my God; I will exalt you and praise your name, for in perfect faithfulness you have done marvelous things, things planned long ago." Isaiah 25:1 (NIV)
41. "Always giving thanks to God the Father for everything, in the name of our Lord Jesus Christ." Ephesians 5:20 (NIV)
42. "Give thanks in all circumstances, for this is God's will for you in Christ Jesus."
1 Thessalonians 5:18 (NIV)

CHAPTER 10: Experiencing God's Presence

43. "The Lord replied, My Presence will go with you, and I will give you rest."
Exodus 33:14 (NIV)

44. "I am still confident of this: I will see the goodness of the Lord in the land of the living." Psalms 27:13 (NIV)

45. "You will seek me and find me when you seek me with all your heart." Jeremiah 29:13 (NIV)

46. "Blessed are the pure in heart, for they will see God." Matthew 5:8 (NIV)

47. "Jesus Christ is the same yesterday, and today and forever." Hebrews 13:8 (NIV)

CHAPTER 11: Never Worry, Doubt or Fear

48. "I sought the Lord, and he answered me; he delivered me from all my fears."
Psalms 34:4 (NIV)
49. "He who dwells in the shelter of the Most High will rest in the shadow of the Almighty..."
Psalms 91 (NIV)
50. "Say to those with fearful hearts; be strong; do not fear; your God will come; he will come with vengeance; with divine retribution, he will come to save you." Isaiah 35:4 (NIV)
51. "Jesus replied, I will tell you the truth, if you have faith and do not doubt, not only can you do what was done to the fig tree, but also you can say to this mountain, go throw yourself into the sea and it will be done." Matthew 21:21 (NIV)
52. "Peace I leave with you; my peace I give you. I do not give to you as the world gives. Do not let your hearts be troubled and do not be afraid."
John 14:27 (NIV)
53. "For I am convinced that neither death nor life, neither angels nor demons, neither the present

nor the future, nor any powers neither height nor depth, nor anything else in all creation, will be able to separate us from the love of God that is in Christ Jesus our Lord." Romans 8: 38-39 (NIV)
54. "Now faith is being sure of what we hope for and certain of what we do not see..."
Hebrews 11: 1-40 (NIV)
55. "But when he asks, he must believe and not doubt, because he who doubts is like a wave of the sea, blown and tossed by the wind."
James 1:6 (NIV)

CHAPTER 12: Stepping Out On Faith

56. "Be still, and know that I am God; I will be exalted among the nations, I will be exalted in the earth." Psalms 46:10 (NIV)
57. "Have faith in God. Jesus answered. I tell you the truth, if anyone says to this mountain, Go throw yourself into the sea and does not doubt in his heart but believes that what he says will happen, it will be done for him. Therefore I tell

you, whatever you ask for in prayer, believe that you have received it, and it will be yours."
Mark 11:22-24 (NIV)

58. "Then Jesus told him, because you have seen me, you have believed; blessed are those who have not seen and yet believed."
John 20:29 (NIV)

59. "Consequently, faith comes from hearing the message, and the message is heard through the word of Christ." Romans 10:17 (NIV)

60. "I can do everything through him who gives me strength." Philippians 4:13 (NIV)

61. "Now faith is being sure of what we hope for and certain of what we do not see…"
Hebrews 11: 1-6 (NIV)

CHAPTER 13: Dreams Come True

62. "For surely, O Lord, you bless the righteous; you surround them with your favor as with a shield." Psalms 5:12 (NIV)
63. "The Lord will guide you always; he will satisfy your needs in a sun-scorched land and will strengthen your frame. You will be like a well-watered garden like a spring whose waters never fail." Isaiah 58: 11 (NIV)
64. "For I know the plans I have for you, declares the Lord, plans to prosper you and give you hope and a future." Jeremiah 29:11 (NIV)
65. "The days are coming, declares the Lord, when the reaper will be overtaken by the plowman and the planter by the one treading grapes. New wine will drip from the mountains and flow from all the hills." Amos 9:13 (NIV)
66. "Jesus looked at them and said, with man this is impossible, but with God all things are possible." Matthew 19:26 (NIV)
67. "Jesus replied, what is impossible with men is possible with God." Luke 18:27 (NIV)

68. "However it is written, No one has seen, no ear has heard, no mind has conceived what God has prepared for those who love him."
1 Corinthians 2:9 (NIV)
69. "Now unto him that is able to do exceedingly abundantly above all that we ask or think, according to the power worketh in us."
Ephesians 3:20 (KJV)

CHAPTER 14: Waiting On God or Is God Waiting On You?

70. "Wait for the Lord; be strong and take heart and wait for the lord." Psalms 27:14 (NIV)
71. "But those who hope in the Lord will renew their strength. They will soar on wings like eagles; they will run and not grow weary, they will walk and not be faint." Isaiah 40:31 (NIV)
72. "For the vision is yet for an appointed time, but at the end it shall speak, and not lie; though it tarry, wait for it; because it will surely come, it will not tarry." Habakkuk 2:3 (KJV)

73. "Let us not become weary in doing good, for at the proper time we will reap a harvest if we do not give up." Galatians 6:9 (NIV)

74. "For we are God's workmanship, created in Christ Jesus to do good works, which God prepared in advance for us to do." Ephesians 2:10 (NIV)

CHAPTER 15: His Will, His Way, His Perfect Timing

75. "He has made everything beautiful in its time. He has also set eternity in the hearts of men; yet they cannot fathom what God has done from beginning to end." Ecclesiastes 3:11 (NIV)

76. "But those who hope in the Lord will renew their strength. They will soar on wings like eagles; they will run and not grow weary, they will walk and not faint." Isaiah 40:31 (NIV)

77. "For the vision is yet for an appointed time, but at the end it shall speak, and not lie; though it tarry, wait for it; because it will surely come, it will not tarry." Habakkuk 2:3 (KJV)

78. "Jesus looked at them and said, with man this is impossible, but with God all things are possible." Matthew 19:26 (NIV)
79. "Be joyful in hope, patient in affliction, faithful in prayer." Romans 12:12 (NIV)
80. "Let us not become weary in doing good, for at the proper time we will reap a harvest if we do not give up." Galatians 6:9 (NIV)

CHAPTER 16: God's Sense of Humor

81. "You will laugh at destruction and famine, and need not fear the beasts of the earth."
Job 5:22 (NIV)
82. "He that sitteth in the heavens shall laugh: the Lord shall have them in derision."
Psalms 2:4 (KJV)
83. "But you, O Lord, laugh at them; you scoff at all those nations." Psalms 59:8 (NIV)
84. "A cheerful heart is good medicine, but a crushed spirit dries up the bones."
Proverbs 17:22 (NIV)

85. "She is clothed with strength and dignity; she can laugh at the days to come."
Proverbs 31:25 (NIV)

CHAPTER 17: God's Pleasure and Delight in You

86. "For God takes delight in his people; he crowns the humble with salvation."
Psalms 149:4 (NIV)
87. "Before I formed you in the womb I knew you, before you were born I set you apart; I appointed you as a prophet to the nations."
Jeremiah 1:5 (NIV)
88. "The Lord your God is with you, he is mighty to save. He will take delight in you, he will quiet you with his love, he will rejoice over you with singing." Zephaniah 3:17 (NIV)
89. "Do not be afraid, little flock, for your father has been pleased to give you the kingdom."
Luke 12:32 (NIV)

90. "No, in all these things we are more than conquerors through him who loved us." Romans 8:37 (NIV)

91. "However it is written, No eye has seen, no ear has heard, no mind has conceived what God has prepared for those who love him." 1 Corinthians 2:9 (NIV)

92. "But the fruit of the Spirit is love, joy, peace, longsuffering, gentleness, goodness, faith, meekness, temperance; against such there is no law." Galatians 5:22-23 (KJV)

93. "He will wipe away every tear from their eyes. There will be no more death or mourning or crying or pain, for the old order of things has passed away." Revelation 21:4 (NIV)

CLOSING:

94. "The Lord bless you and watch, guard and keep you. The Lord make his face to shine upon you and enlighten you and be gracious to you. The Lord lift up his countenance upon you and give you peace." Numbers 6: 24-26 (NIV)

ACKNOWLEDGEMENTS

I'm so grateful for all my family and friends who God have placed in my life. The prayers, encouraging words and support are deeply appreciated.

I'm especially and forever grateful for my mommy, Martha Maclin Reynolds. God has blessed me to have the best mommy in the world. No matter what, she has always been my greatest encourager with her unconditional love, encouraging words, Godly wisdom, approachable demeanor, firm correction and a sense of humor that will keep you entertained. Thank you for always showing me what a mother's love feels like.

I would like to thank my dear sister, friend, Robin Phillips. Our friendship was an instant connection and has evolved into a special, sisterly bond. Her spirituality and relaxed persona are infectious. Thank you for your listening ear and wonderful laughs just when I needed them most.

I would like to thank my cousin, Sean Wilson. His spiritual, encouraging words and teachings are with me daily. Sean, being an author and pastor, inspired and motivated me to complete my book. Observing him, I saw that with God all things are possible. Thank you, Sean, for sharing your expertise in this area and giving freely of yourself. I deeply appreciate all you've done.

I would like to thank my boys, Joshua and Jordan. The encouraging words and love that they consistently express to me keep me striving forward. I love you both unconditionally and more than life. Thank you for the laughs and your understanding throughout this entire process.

I would like to thank my brother and father, Senam and Sam Maclin and my stepfather, Erwin Savage. Thank you for always loving and supporting me.

Lastly, I would like to thank God, my Father. I thank you, God, for having patience with me, loving me unconditionally and for Your supernatural abundance of Your favor, grace and mercy that You give me simply because You love me.

In Jesus' Name, Amen!!!!

www.ingramcontent.com/pod-product-compliance
Lightning Source LLC
Chambersburg PA
CBHW060402050426
42449CB00009B/1864